YOUR KNOWLEDGE HAS VALUE

Cross-border insolvency proceedings

Regulation (EU) 2015/848

Anika Petzold

Bibliographic information published by the German National Library:

The German National Library lists this publication in the National Bibliography; detailed bibliographic data are available on the Internet at http://dnb.dnb.de.

ISBN: 9783389055656
This book is also available as an ebook.

© GRIN Publishing GmbH
Trappentreustraße 1
80339 München

Print and binding: Books on Demand GmbH, Norderstedt, Germany
Printed on acid-free paper from responsible sources.

The present work has been carefully prepared. Nevertheless, authors and publishers do not incur liability for the correctness of information, notes, links and advice as well as any printing errors.

GRIN web shop: https://www.grin.com/document/1496338

Assessment

Regulation (EU) 2015/848 of the European Parliament and of the Council of 20 May 2015 on insolvency proceedings

Faculty of Business Law (LL.M.)

presented by

Anika Petzold

European and international reorganization and insolvency law - legal status 08/2023

Contents

Bibliography

McCormack, Gerard, EU Insolvency Law – Cross-Border Insolvency Law in
　　Comparative Focus, Edward Elgar Publishing Limited
　　(British Library – Library of Congress Control Number: 2022941185)

Kindler, Peter, (Hrsg.) Kindler/Nachmann/Bitzer, Handbuch Insolvenzrecht in Europa,
　　13. EL Februar 2023

Knof, Belá, (Ed.) Hirte/Vallender, Uhlenbruck, Insolvenzordnung: InsO, EuInsVO,
　　SanInsKG und StaRUG, 16. Auflage 2023

List of sources

Internet resources list

URL 1: Gesamter Siemens-Bericht
Gesamter Siemens-Bericht

https://www.siemens.com/applications/b09c49eb-3a14-73b3-9f71-
e30e3c2dfdbd/s3_assets/pdfs/de/Siemens_Bericht_GJ2022.pdf?ste_sid=f69396c0b7
24888843b65519640666e9

(last access on 12.08.2023)

URL 2: Jahresabschluss der Siemens AG zum 30. September 2020
Jahresabschluss der Siemens AG zum 30. September 2020

https://assets.new.siemens.com/siemens/assets/api/uuid:f869ecb2-bc2b-46ab-9fcc-
87e2fdd646a3/siemens-sag2020-D.pdf

(last access on 12.08.2023)

URL 3: Siemens Osakeyhtiö und MaaS Global Oy kooperieren bei Pilotprojekt in
Tampere | Suchergebnisse | Unternehmen | Siemens, online at:
Siemens Osakeyhtiö und MaaS Global Oy kooperieren bei Pilotprojekt in
Tampere | Suchergebnisse | Unternehmen | Siemens

https://press.siemens.com/fi/fi/lehdistotiedote/siemens-osakeyhtio-ja-maas-global-oy-
yhteistyohon-tampereelle-
toteutettavaan#:~:text=Siemens%20Osakeyhti%C3%B6ll%C3%A4%20on%20kiinteis
t%C3%B6jen%20digitaalisia%20palveluja%20tarjoava%20VIBECO-
tyt%C3%A4ryhti%C3%B6,215%20miljoonaa%20euroa%20ja%20henkil%C3%B6st%
C3%B6n%20m%C3%A4%C3%A4r%C3%A4%20noin%20535.

(last access on 12.08.2023)

List of Databases

Beck-online.de (database used), online at:

Homepage - beck-online

https://beck-online.beck.de/Home   *(last access on 12.08.2023)*

List of Abbreviations

acc.	in accordance with / according to
AG /plc	Public limited company
Art.	Article
c.f./comp.	confer / compare
COMI	Center of Main Interest
ECJ	European Court of Justice (EuGH)
e.d.	Editor / editors
Ed.	Edition
e.g.	exempli gratia
etc.	et cetera
EG	European Community
ECJ	European Court of Justice (ECJ)
EEA countries	EWR-States (Island, Liechtenstein, Norway)
EIR / EuInsVO	Regulation (EU) 2015/848 of the European Parliament and of the Council of 20 May 2015 on Insolvency Proceedings (EIR)
EL	Supplementary delivery
EU	European Union
EUR	Euro
ff./cont.	continued
i.c.w.	in conjunction with
i.s.o.	in the sense of
InsO	Insolvency Code
No.	number
par.	Paragraph
purs.	pursuant to
P./p.	Page
rec.	recital
resp.	respectively
Reg.	Regulation
Rn.	Recital (Randnummer)

Rome I	Regulation (EC) No 593/2008 of the European Parliament and of the Council of 17 June 2008 on the law applicable to contractual obligations (Rome I)
s.a.	see also
sec.	sequence
subpar.	subparagraph
S.	sentence
StaRUG	Act on the Stabilization and Restructuring Framework for Companies (Unternehmensstabilisierungs- und restrukturierungsgesetz – StaRUG)
UNCITRAL	United Nations Commission on International Trade Law
ZIP	Zeitschrift für Wirtschaftsrecht (Journal of Business Law)

1 Introduction

The following explanations include the objectives as well as the scope and special features of the Regulation (EU) 2015/848 of the European Parliament and of the Council of 20 May 2015 on insolvency proceedings (EuInsVO/EIR) which are illustrated by means of a practical example.

2 Objectives of the regulation

In times of international globalization, a smooth functioning of the internal market and efficient as well as effective cross-border insolvency proceedings are required, which will be standardized within the EU with the help of the Regulation. This is intended to prevent the relocation of assets or legal proceedings to different member states in the event of insolvency in order to exploit legal advantages ("Forum Shopping") to the detriment of creditors.

Regulation (EU) 2015/848 is intended to coordinate insolvency proceedings between the European Member States and bundle provisions on the place of jurisdiction and on the applicable law in order to prevent forum shopping. In this respect, a distinction has to be made in advance as to whether the facts of the case have a foreign connection within or outside the EU. Furthermore, significant case law (e.g. Eurofood, Parmalat) should also be noted in this context, which are presented in the following.

3 Insolvency law cross-border issues

3.1 Outside the EU (Matters relating to foreign countries (Third Countries)

For insolvency law cross-border issues outside the EU §§ 335 ff. InsO shall apply accordingly (international insolvency law). The provision stipulates that the insolvency proceedings and their effects are governed by the law of the State in which the proceedings were opened. With respect to contracts with rights in rem in immovable property, the effects of insolvency proceedings shall be governed by the law of the State in which the property is located (place of location) pursuant to § 336 InsO. Similar to the EU regulation, the Model Law of UNCITRAL contains regulations on a global scale[1], e.g. for preserving assets and creditor protection; which major trading partner are the Unites States of America.

---

[1] McCormack, Gerard, EU Insolvency Law – Cross-Border Insolvency Law in Comparative Focus, p.1.

3.2 Inside the EU (Matters relating to foreign countries (EU-countries)

Inside the EU the regulation applies, if the material, spatial-personal and temporal scope is opened. The main proceedings will be opened in the Member State, where the debtor has the center of his main interests (COMI). The goal is universal application (principle of universality) for the protection of all creditors and coverage of all assets within the European Union (rec. 23).

Insolvency proceedings and their effects shall be governed by the law of the Member State within the territory of which the proceedings are opened (Art. 7 par. 1 and par. 2 EIR i.c.w. Rome I (Regulation (EG) Nr. 593/2008). The Regulation does not affect the rights in rem of a creditor or a third party to the debtor's tangible, intangible, movable or immovable property that is in the territory of another Member State at the time when insolvency proceedings are opened (Art. 8 par. 1 EIR).

The Regulation permits the opening of secondary insolvency proceedings (Art. 34 EIR) in parallel with the main insolvency proceedings in order to protect different interests (rec. 23). However, secondary insolvency proceedings may be opened only in the Member State in which the debtor has its establishment. The effects of the secondary insolvency proceedings are limited to the assets located in the Member State.

If a German court does not have jurisdiction, but the debtor has an establishment or other assets in Germany, the opening of individual proceedings shall be requested by a creditor (Art. 354 par. 1 InsO).

The territorial proceedings become secondary insolvency proceedings after the main insolvency proceedings have been opened (Art. 3 par. 2 S. 2 EIR).

A single insolvency administrator is appointed for each insolvency proceeding. Within a group of companies, group coordination proceedings may be opened upon request by the competent court purs. to Art. 63 par. 1 EIR in conjunction with Art. 68 par. 1 EIR provided that all requirements for this are met.

4 Scope of application of the EIR (Reg. 2015/848)

Inside the EU the Regulation (EU) 2015/848 applies, if the material, temporal scope and spatial-personal is opened[2].

4.1 Material scope

The material scope of application is opened according to Art. 1 (1) subpar. 1 EIR, if:

---

[2] s.a. McCormack, EU Insolvency Law – Cross-Border Insolvency Law in Comparative Focus, p. 6,7.

a) the debtor has been deprived of the power of disposal over his assets in whole or in part and an administrator has been appointed,

b) the debtor's assets and business are placed under judicial control or supervision, or

c) a temporary stay of individual enforcement proceedings is granted by a court or by operation of law.

There are exceptions to the material scope of application pursuant to Art. 1 (2) of the EU-Regulation (e.g. for credit institutions, insurance companies)[3].

4.2 Temporal scope

The EIR applies from 26 June 2017 (Art. 92 subpar. 2 EIR) or from the 20th day after its publication in the Official Journal of the European Union (Art. 92 subpar. 1 EIR)[4].

4.3 Spatial-personal scope

The spatial-personal scope of application (Art. 3 (1) subpar. 1 EIR) is applied according to the determination of the center of the main interest ("COMI") in an EU-Member State and a cross-border insolvency issue[5] and the principles developed by case law, which are explained below on practical example of a quoted listed company (Siemens AG).

5 Determination of COMI – practice example

5.1 Example and problem statement

As described below the Regulation (EU) 2015/848 has direct effect on the Member States, if the material, temporal and spatial-personal scope is opened (purs. Art. 1, Art. 92 and. Art. 3 (1) EIR) under the principle of qualified unity, the principle of qualified universality, subjection of proceedings, recognition of judgement and conferment of power to "main proceedings" liquidator. Member States in the sense of the EIR means all European Member States excluding Denmark[6] and the EEA countries (EWR-States).

If, for example, the German listed Siemens AG (headquarter Munich) becomes insolvent with its worldwide and wholly owned EU-subsidiaries (e.g. Siemens

---

[3] McCormack, EU Insolvency Law – Cross-Border Insolvency Law in Comparative Focus, p. 6.

[4] Knof, (Ed.) Uhlenbruck, Insolvenzordnung: InsO, EuInsO, SanInsKG und StaRUG, 16. Auflage 2023, VO (EU) 2015/848 Art. 3 International Zuständigkeit, Rn. 1.

[5] Knof, (Ed.) Uhlenbruck, Insolvenzordnung: InsO, EuInsO, SanInsKG und StaRUG, 16. Auflage 2023, VO (EU) 2015/848 Art. 3 International Zuständigkeit, Rn. 2.

[6] s.a. McCormack, Gerard, EU Insolvency Law – Cross-Border Insolvency Law in Comparative Focus, p. 6.

Osakeyhtiö, Espoo/Finland), it is questionable where the center of main interest ("COMI") is located of these globally operating group within the meaning of Art. 3 (1) subpar. 1 S. 2 i.c.w. subpar. 2 EIR, which law will be applicable, where the insolvency proceedings take place and who assumes the power of administration and disposition as insolvency administrator. Furthermore, it is important to which court the creditors can turn in order to assert or sue for their claims, where the assets are located and, to a significant extent, where they can be found. The Reg. 2015/848 does not apply, resp. the spatial-personal scope is not opened for the Danish wholly owned subsidiary (Siemens A/S, Ballerup; Denmark), because Denmark didn´t adopt the Regulation[7].

In a first step the meaning of "insolvency" will be defined by a balance sheet test and a cash flow test. The Siemens AG will be insolvent, as soon as the liabilities exceeds its assets in the balance sheet (over-indebtedness) or the Siemens AG will be unable to pay its debts when they fall due (insolvency); both circumstances may exist. The material scope is opened because of the cross-border issue within the EU and the temporal scope (purs. Art. 92 EIR) as well. The spatial-personal scope will be determined based on the COMI.

The center of main interest is presumed (purs. Art. 3 (1) subpar. 1 S. 2 EIR) as, "the place where the debtor habitually pursues the management of his interests and which is ascertainable by third parties" (s.a. recital 28). For legal persons the presumption exists, the COMI is located at registered office (Art. 3 (1) subpar. 2 S. 1 EIR).

5.2 Ascertainment of the COMI

Due to a lack of legal definition of the COMI, problems have regularly arisen in the ascertainment of the COMI in individual cases. In rec. 13 EIR (old version) contained the assumption that the "center of the debtor's main interests" (COMI) "should be deemed to be the place where the debtor habitually pursues the management of his interests and is thus ascertainable by third parties"[8]. This specification is legally defined in Art. 3 (1) subpar. 1 S. 2 i.c.w. Art. 3 (2) EIR in the course of the reform of the ECJ Regulation and has thus taken on the character of a norm.[9] Therefore, theories and legal principles for determining the COMI have been developed by the courts over the years[10]. Furthermore, special features arise in the case of a group insolvency of a globally operating listed company (e.g. Siemens AG). The court of the Member State,

---

[7] Knof, (Ed.) Uhlenbruck, Insolvenzordnung: InsO, EuInsO, SanInsKG und StaRUG, 16. Auflage 2023, VO (EU) 2015/848 Art. 3 International Zuständigkeit, Rn. 3.

[8] c.f. Knof, (Ed.) Uhlenbruck, Insolvenzordnung: InsO, EuInsO, SanInsKG und StaRUG, 16. Auflage 2023, VO (EU) 2015/848 Art. 3 International Zuständigkeit, Rn. 6.

[9] Knof, (Ed.) Uhlenbruck, Insolvenzordnung: InsO, EuInsO, SanInsKG und StaRUG, 16. Auflage 2023, VO (EU) 2015/848 Art. 3 Internationale Zuständigkeit, Rn. 6.

[10] McCormack, EU Insolvency Law – Cross-Border Insolvency Law in Comparative Focus, p. 10.

which is responsible for opening the insolvency proceedings (main insolvency proceedings) is decisive in this respect (recital 23 VO (EU) 2015/848). Changes of jurisdiction will arise to another EU-Member State (rebuttable) by movement within the last three months before request of opening the proceedings (Art. 3 par. 1 subpar. 2 S. 2 EIR). The two principles of the EIR imply normally at first the COMI in that EU-Member State, where the COMI is situated ("main proceedings"-place of the registered office- in the example the COMI for Siemens would be in Munich/ Germany) or second where the debtor company has an establishment ("territorial proceedings"- in the example in Espoo/Finland).

Siemens AG has the particularity of two places of registered offices in Berlin (place of establishment) and Munich. Background was the separation of Germany in consequence of the second world war. Insofar, Munich is the youngest registered office (also address of the international corporate group) and the COMI of the registered office of the Siemens AG is in Germany; creditors can turn there in order to assert or sue for their claims.

However, the assumption of COMI at the registered offices (Berlin/Munich) of the company is valid only until proven otherwise[11]. The court has to examine ex officio which interests of the debtor are central and where these are located (Art. 4 (1) EIR). International jurisdiction for opening secondary or partial insolvency proceedings is linked to the place of establishment of the debtor.[12]

Principles and presumptions changed the presumptions of Unity (Qualified Unity for local creditors with access to local assets) and Universality (Qualified Universality -main proceedings encompass the whole worldwide assets of the debtor) in consequence of case law. The most famous named ECJ-jurisdiction has been Eurofood/Parmalat and few more[13]. Hence, it is still questionable and to ascertain, where the COMI of the Siemens AG (parent company) will be located in an insolvency proceeding in consideration of the case law.

5.3 Jurisdiction

Regarding the interpretation of Art. 3 (1) EIR for determining the COMI three fundamental ECJ case law judgements does exist in order to rebut the presumption of Art. 3 (1) subpar. 2 S. 1 i.c.w. Art. 3 (1) S. 2 EIR.

---

[11] Knof, (Ed.) Uhlenbruck, Insolvenzordnung: InsO, EuInsO, SanInsKG und StaRUG, 16. Auflage 2023, VO (EU) 2015/848 Art. 3 International Zuständigkeit, Rn. 23.

[12] Knof, (Ed.) Uhlenbruck, Insolvenzordnung: InsO, EuInsO, SanInsKG und StaRUG, 16. Auflage 2023, VO (EU) 2015/848 Art. 3 International Zuständigkeit, Rn. 23.

[13] e.g. Enron Directo Sociedad Limitad, Crisscross Telecommunications Group, Vierländer Bau Union Ltd., Daistek-Gruppe, Automold etc.

5.3.1 Eurofood / Parmalat

The Eurofood case law judgement[14] contains, that the debtor's registered office normally is decisive for the court's jurisdiction when the insolvency proceedings are opened (mind-of-management-theory)[15]. However, in the context of the collapse of the Parmalat Group, the first fundamental case law of the ECJ[16] developed on the interpretation of the international jurisdiction of Art. 3 (1) subpar. 1 S. 2 EIR[17]. The ECJ developed assumptions for determining the COMI:

1. Presumption i.s.o. Art. 3 (1) subpar. 1 i.c.w. subpar. 2 EIR

2. The presumption can be rebutted by the debtor

   a) on the basis of objective factors (provable) and

   b) these factors must be ascertainable by third parties

   Third parties must be able to notice the different COMI instead of the registered office[18].

3. Enabling a different COMI from the located COMI of the registered office; in result the presumption is rebutted ("business-activity theory")[19]

4. Full economic control from a parent company over a subsidiary is not enough for rebutting the presumption the COMI on the registered office.

Regarding the Parmalat case law decision, the court judged the ascertainment by third parties in the judgement case of an Irish limited company at the registered office of the parent group company in Italy. The company was only founded for financing transactions of them and in addition the parent group company has assumed a payment guarantee to the creditors of the financing company[20]. The opening of the insolvency proceeding was rejected from Ireland to Italy within the scope of the examination of the competence ex officio (pur. Art. 4 (1) S. 1 EIR).

In the example, the COMI of Siemens AG (registered office in Munich/Berlin) does not automatically change to Espoo/Finland, because of the one hundred percent wholly owned contribution and economic power over the Siemens Osakeyhtiö[21]. In a first step, the COMI is still at the registered office of the

---

[14] ECJ, Judgement from 02.05.2006 – C-341/04 Eurofood IFSC Ltd., NZI 2006, p. 360.

[15] Knof, (Ed.) Uhlenbruck, Insolvenzordnung: InsO, EuInsO, SanInsKG und StaRUG, 16. Auflage 2023, VO (EU) 2015/848 Art. 3 International Zuständigkeit, Rn. 42.

[16] ECJ-Judgement from 02/05/2006 - 341-04, NZI 2006, p. 360.

[17] Kindler,(Ed.) Kindler/Nachmann/Bitzer, Handbuch Insolvenzrecht in Europa, 13. EL Februar 2023, Rn. 42.

[18] Knof, (Ed.) Uhlenbruck, Insolvenzordnung: InsO, EuInsO, SanInsKG und StaRUG, 16. Auflage 2023, VO (EU) 2015/848 Art. 3 International Zuständigkeit, Rn. 28.

[19] comp. Knof, (Ed.) Uhlenbruck, Insolvenzordnung: InsO, EuInsO, SanInsKG und StaRUG, 16. Auflage 2023, VO (EU) 2015/848 Art. 3 International Zuständigkeit, Rn. 30.

[20] Tribunale di Parma vom 19/02/2004 – 53/04, FHZivR 50 Nr. 8329.

[21] Knof, (Ed.) Uhlenbruck, Insolvenzordnung: InsO, EuInsO, SanInsKG und StaRUG, 16. Auflage 2023, VO (EU) 2015/848 Art. 3 International Zuständigkeit, Rn. 29.

Siemens AG in Germany purs. Art. 3 (1) subpar. 2 S. 1 EIR unless the presumption can be rebutted based on the above listed assumptions.

5.3.2 BRAC

The jurisdiction listed above was confirmed by the case law judgement BRAC[22], but with this decision the so called "automatic-stay" have been developed. The main insolvency proceedings will be opened in the place of the administrative headquarters instead of the registered office[23]. In context with the English case law decision it was significant, that the BRAC Rent-A-Car International Inc. (USA) has fallen into the scope of the Reg. 2015/848 although it is not a European Member State[24]. The court decided the COMI in England in the sense of the EIR. The reasoning was the rebutted presumption of Art. 3 (1) subpar. 2 S. 1 i.c.w. Art. 3 (1) subpar. 1 S. 2 EIR because of their operating business in England. Furthermore, no employees were engaged in the United States and the contract law with establishments were agreed under English law.

5.3.3 COMI of Siemens AG

In the example, we have to investigate the located administrative headquarter of Siemens AG -in compliance with the case law- in order to determine the COMI for rebutting the presumption i.s.o. Art. 3 (1) subpar. 2 S. 1 EIR (registered office). Considering the Parmalat case law it contains a comprehensive assessment of all relevant facts and circumstances. Also, the objective figure, if the Siemens company does not carry on any business in the territory of the Member State of his registered office in Munich/Berlin. The objective figures includes the actual center of management and supervision and of the management of its interest. These objective figures must be ascertain for all third parties (especially creditors/stakeholders)[25].

The segment report of Siemens AG includes Digital Industries, Smart Infrastructure, Mobility and Siemens Healthineers as well Siemens Financial Services[26]. The Siemens AG itself employs appr. over 100.000 employees and generated sales itself of 16.389 Mio. EUR in 2020[27]. The company has his own operating business in Germany. Supervisory Board and Executive Board are mainly located in Munich (as well in Berlin). These objectives figures are located in Germany and are ascertain to third parties. The presumption of Art.

---

[22] ECJ from 14/1/2003, ZIP 2003, Rn. 813.
[23] Knof, (Ed.) Uhlenbruck, Insolvenzordnung: InsO, EuInsO, SanInsKG und StaRUG, 16. Auflage 2023, VO (EU) 2015/848 Art. 3 International Zuständigkeit, Rn. 47.
[24] McCormack, EU Insolvency Law – Cross-Border Insolvency Law in Comparative Focus, p. 10.
[25] Knof, (Ed.) Uhlenbruck, Insolvenzordnung: InsO, EuInsO, SanInsKG und StaRUG, 16. Auflage 2023, VO (EU) 2015/848 Art. 3 International Zuständigkeit, Rn. 34.
[26] URL 1: Gesamter Siemens-Bericht.
[27] URL 2: Jahresabschluss der Siemens AG zum 30. September 2020.

3 par. 1 subpar. 2 S. 2 EIR cannot rebutted, in result the COMI of Siemens AG is located in Munich/Berlin (registered office/headquarter).

The Finnish company Siemens Osakeyhtiö was not only founded for financing transactions and is an independent company with a subsidiary (VIBECO). Siemens Osakeyhtiö offers solutions, services and products for sustainable energy production and employs approx. 535 employees and generates sales of approx. 215 million EUR[28]. Into account of the Eurofood jurisdiction, the COMI of Siemens Osakeyhtiö is not automatically on the registered office of the parent company Siemens AG in Germany, compared to the Eurofood ECJ case law and reverse the operating business of the Siemens AG is not exclusively exercised by the Finnish company.

In result the German court has jurisdiction acc. Art. 1 subpar. 1 S. 1 EIR i.c.w. Art. 3 subpar. 2 S. 1 EIR for insolvency proceedings and the applicable law is German law acc. Art. 7 (1) i.c.w. Art. 7 (2) EIR.

6 Conclusion

The Regulation (EU) 2015/848 harmonized the European insolvency law between all the Member States because of uniform rules regarding cross-border insolvency proceedings. The aim, to avoid bogus companies in order to move assets in other countries at the expense of creditors or to affect the International jurisdiction by relocation of registered office could thus be implemented within the EU. This was most recently confirmed by the case law (ECJ, Judgement from 24.03.2023 – C-723/20).

---

[28] URL 2: The finnish company Siemens Osakeyhtiö was not only founded for financing transactions and is an independent company with a subsidiary (VIBECO).

YOUR KNOWLEDGE HAS VALUE

- We will publish your bachelor's and master's thesis, essays and papers

- Your own eBook and book - sold worldwide in all relevant shops

- Earn money with each sale

Upload your text at www.GRIN.com
and publish for free